FEATHERS, STARS, AND MOONLIGHT

a colouring book of winged horses

SUGGESTED MATERIALS

Each image is printed on its own sheet of paper and various materials can be used to colour them in. As each image has its own page, they can all be torn out and framed.

We recommend coloured pencils, crayons, metallic pens, indian ink, and watercolours or other paints used slightly more dryly than normal.

Whatever you are using, it is best to place a sheet of thick paper or card beneath your image as you work, to protect the following page from potential bleed through. Permanent marker pens, for example, will almost certainly bleed through.

Please use the following blank pages as a place to test your chosen materials.

The delicate images make use of bold lines contrasted with empty space, to allow your own creative input. You could colour the images in as they stand or add extra line detail (for example, by filling a background with stars or adding zebra stripes to a horse's face). Images could become colourful rainbows or elegant monochromatic patterns.

PRACTICE PAGES – test out your colouring and line drawing materials here.

PRACTICE PAGES – test out your colouring and line drawing materials here.

"O, for a horse with wings!"

~ William Shakespeare, "Cymbeline"

The winged horses are made of moonlight and are hidden all around us.

When moonbeams hit frost, stars, or branches, the light scatters, shatters, and bursts into rainbows, revealing long limbs, wild manes, large dark eyes, and gleaming feathers. If you're very quiet, and very careful, you can see them at the stroke of twelve on cold, cloudless nights.

The winged horses change their appearance all the time. They can be gold, silver, blue, pink... Some are covered in snowflakes, stars, or splashes of colour. When a winged horse wants to change its coat, it swims beneath a waterfall at midnight. The glittering drops of water burst against its wings making colourful prisms, and when it emerges and shakes off the spray it has transformed. They are a little vain, and enjoy looking at their reflections in pools and puddles.

The wind always blows in their world. It tickles their feathers and lifts their wings, letting them fly above mountains and seas. They are gentle, friendly beasts and are usually found flying in pairs or threes, showing off their tricks to one another. They like to sleep curled up in snow or underneath leafless trees. All horses become winged horses one day and they can hear their feathered brothers and sisters even when we can't. This is why horses often look into the distance or leap for joy on windy days.

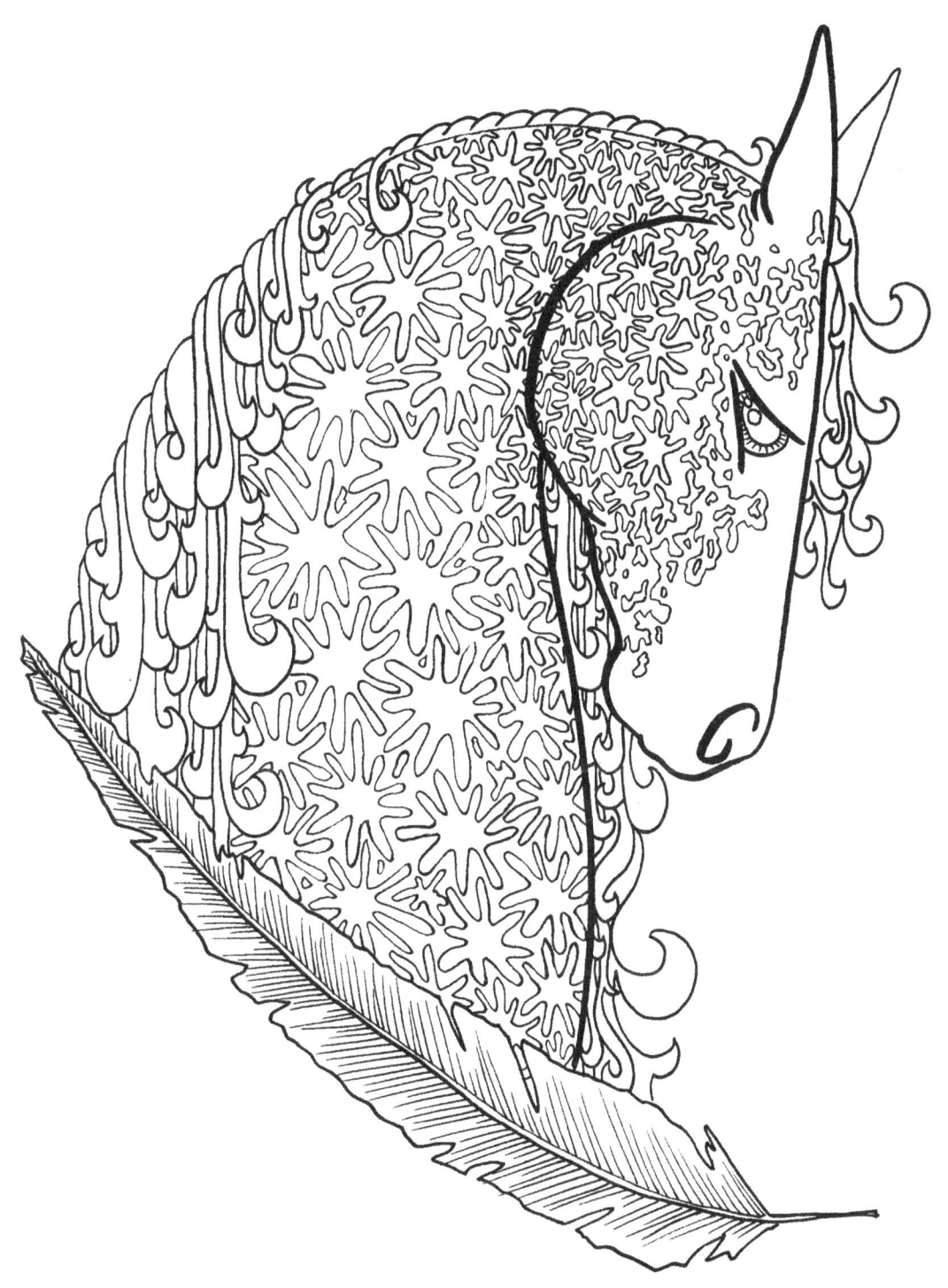

www.ingramcontent.com/pod-product-compliance
Lightning Source LLC
Chambersburg PA
CBHW081559280526
45788CB00011B/3512